AF254767

Effective Parenting

A practical understanding of child up-bringing

By: Vanessa Boateng-Ukoro

Vanessa Boateng-Ukoro

Effective Parenting

A practical understanding of child up-bringing

© 2019 Vanessa Boateng-Ukoro

ISBN: 978-1-9160102-0-8

Copyright © 2019 New Era Initiative

Liverpool, United Kingdom. All Rights Reserved

Effective Parenting – A practical understanding of child up-bringing – Liverpool, United Kingdom:

New Era Initiative, 2019

Dedication

This book is dedicated to my Creator, in whom I live, move and have my total being. To my loving and supportive husband – Felix Othuke Ukoro for encouraging and believing in me as I took up the bold decision to write this book. To my lovely children Nanayaw, Benjamin and Joanna who inspired me to write this book in my parenting journey.

Acknowledgment

I wish to acknowledge my appreciation to my friends, colleagues and family for encouraging my work with parents. I sincerely wish to acknowledge my mother Mrs. Blessing Boateng for her enormous support and advice and believing in me. I also acknowledge my mentor Dr. Sunday Adeleja for his support and encouragement in putting my experiences and knowledge into this book. Finally, to a friend, Pauline Pani Limen, for believing in my content and my capability in this wonderful venture.

About The Author

Vanessa Boateng-Ukoro is a Speaker, Philanthropist and a Parent Mentor. She is passionate about holistic family relationships, and the welfare and protection of children. She believes that the family is the backbone of every society and there are underlying factors that make families successful to create a better society.

She shares practical strategies parents can implement in the upbringing of their children at various events and one to one therapeutic sessions. Her work has been proven and tested by various local authorities in the UK and has gained recognition by Her Royal Majesty Queen Elizabeth II on her contribution to the Commonwealth Diaspora community in the UK. She is married and a mother of three children, and is currently studying Social Policy Combined with Childhood and Youth at the Liverpool Hope University.

Preface

The purpose of this book is to empower and equip parents with the necessary tools needed to help them become better at their parental skills and journey. In my 18 years of being a parent and a Sunday school teacher, I have encountered a lot of parents who are struggling with their behavioral management skills in parenting their children. Most people are not equipped on how to handle children when they start having children.

They depend on how they were brought up and the majority of the time it seems not to work which causes a lot of frustration. There is a famous saying by a friend which is – you cannot use an analogous mode of thinking to raise a digital child. In my interaction with parents, I have found out that most of them would appreciate a form of guidance in helping them to become more effective in their parenting skills.

Some parents have low self-esteem challenges which affect the way they relate with their children and regrettably, this is having a huge impact on the children in today's society. Some parents do not see the need to be involved in their children's emotional well-being or have little or no understanding of how their behavior management has an impact on the well-being of their children. My greatest motivation in writing this book is my desire to see children and parents in healthy relationships for a bright future. Why effective parenting? It is my inspiration that every parent is can be Effective in their parenting skills.

Effective in the sense that parenting is less stressful when the fundamentals are solid and children are brought up in a structured manner. Parenting is not about power, but in our children's eyes, it can be. What our children view as power, we know is a respect issue. As parents, our job is to teach our children to respect us and God. I must acknowledge the contribution of my mentor Dr. Sunday Adelaja who has contributed immensely to the material content of this book.

Foreword

This is not just a book; I would say this is a book about what every parent would like to know about parenting. Everything you should know about parenting is in this book and I am amazed at how practical it is. I can only say that probably the secret of this book is the fact that it is written first of all, from the perspective of a mother. Vanessa is a mother and you can see it from the touch of the book and the questions raised in it.

The practicality of this book makes it a dream book of all parents, I would say. If you know anyone who is getting ready to have a child or is already parenting a child, there is no way you should set out parenting without having to read this book; both for males and females, mothers and fathers. This book would open your eyes big time to get you ready to what it means to be a father or a mother, to understand your children and be able to raise the best children in the world to the glory of God.

Vanessa Boateng-Ukoro has done a great, great job. This is a legacy book. This book would become a legacy for years to come. It would outlive the author and would be a reference for future parents and children unborn. Thank you so much, Vanessa, for taking out time to sit down and put together such a book for the world.

Dr. Sunday Adelaja

Kiev, Ukraine

Contents

Page Left Blank Intentionally

Chapter 1

Parents: Being and Becoming

What is your purpose of becoming a parent?

I have posed the same question to countless parents that I have come into contact with over the years. I have almost never received a well-thought-out answer. From this, I have concluded that people find it difficult to locate the reasons for becoming parents. This is problematic because being aware of your purpose as a parent is one of, if not the most, crucial aspect of parenting.

How can you be an effective parent? It all begins with knowing the purpose behind your state of parenthood. Ask yourself this question if you haven't already. Your answers will serve as your starting point. Beginning from there, you can use this guide to learn how to effectively raise your children.

From interviewing several people informally, I have come to know that the main purpose of parenting for any parent is to help their child become an independent individual. You, as a parent, would want to help your child examine why he or she was born into the world; to know himself or herself; and to learn the purpose of their existence. So it can be said that the purpose of parenting is to help a child discover himself or herself.

It is to nurture a child so that they may stretch their wings and develop as a human being. Unfortunately, many parents lack the proper understanding to make that happen. They think that the purpose of parenting is restricted to providing for the most basic needs of their children. Parenting is much more than providing food, shelter and clothing for your child.

Parenting extends beyond fulfilling the tangible needs of a child to help take care of their intangible needs. Find out your purpose behind parenting your child. It will be the most fundamental and important foundation on which you can build to become an effective parent. As you learn the 'whys' and the 'hows' of your parenting journey, consider the following parameters of parenthood. These are the few primary aspects that you need to consider and follow to become a better parent:

Character And Core Value System

As a parent, you have to contribute to building the character and core value system of your child. The core value system could be likened to the skeleton of a human being: it forms the structure of the body. As you become a parent, you should have a set of goals and core values of life to pass on to your child.

Before you transfer or inculcate any values in your child, you must be aware of life's value. You must have a purpose behind raising your children in the specific way that you do. You must have an understanding of what you want to pass down to a child. For this reason, you must have a concept of life, which you know is worthwhile. Only when you have a meaningful set of principles by which to live a life that you can hand them down to your child.

I would advise all parents-to-be to have a clear understanding of their core values as an individual before they have children. Unfortunately, there can be no fixed purpose behind parenting; in many ways, the environment determines your parenting style. As a result, children tend to adapt to what they encounter in their environment. If a child is brought up without relying on a strong core value system, the child will embrace the things that they see around themselves.

Your responsibility as a parent is to build a core value system in your child. Parenting is about building a system of character from childhood through adolescence and on to adulthood. You are a parent so your assignment is to help your child build a concrete and definitive value system, which they will hold on to and abide by not only in their childhood but throughout their life.

Parenting, then, can be said to be the ability to build this system in your child so that he or she knows the principles to follow as they live their lives. When you inoculate values in your child, he or she will be able to manage situations, handle challenges, make the right choices and take good decisions. If you instill a sound value system in your children, they will not be swayed by the vices of society. Furthermore, they will be able to defend themselves against peer pressure because they will have a strong sense of right or wrong; they will rely on their learned values to make judgments.

Without a core value system, your child will remain vulnerable to the external world. Core value system and character are what will ground them. So inculcate a core value system in your child and develop their character. For this essentially, will be the figurative spine of your child all through his or her life.

Discovering The Purpose Of Life For Your Child

As a parent, it is your duty to guide your child to understand the purpose of living. You should help your child find their purpose; the next step would be to help them fulfill their purpose. It is vital for you as a parent, to know that you have to assist your child or children in discovering themselves.

You must help your child comprehend their ability to live for a goal and sound purpose. And then, you should help them throughout their journey. Parenting, in this sense, is another name for orienting your child and guiding them in the right direction.

Develop A Governmental Structure In Your Home

Developing a governmental structure in your home will help your children develop an appreciation for law and order. Life is guided by law and order, and it is your primary responsibility as a parent to help your child build these principles in themselves. The basic environment for every child is the home. Equip them on how to carry themselves in the world outside their home. If you do not set up an effective structure of orderliness in the home, you will only set up your child to struggle and then fail in the larger society. Start early and start at home.

Chapter 2

Understanding Your Child In Their Development Stages

To be an effective parent, you need to understand the developmental abilities and limitations of your child at different stages of their life. Most parents go into parenthood without much forethought. You too may have done the same. You may still be raising your child without knowing the changes that he or she experiences when growing up. It is recommended that you familiarize yourself with the stages of child development; it will help you bring up your child in a healthier manner.

Child development envelops the biological as well as psychological and emotional development that human beings experience, from the time of their birth to the conclusion of their adolescence. From the perspective of holistic development, a child exists as a whole person; he or she is an individual with not only physical but also intellectual, emotional, social, as well spiritual and moral needs that must be met during the period of their maturity.

Table of milestones

Age	Motor	Speech	Vision and hearing	Social
1–1.5 months	Holds the head erect and steady when held upright.	Cooes and babbles at parents and people they know.	Focuses on parents.	• Loves looking at new faces. • Starts to smile. at parents • Startled by sudden noises.
1.6–2 months	When prone, lifts self by arms; rolls from side to back.	Vocalizes; Cooes (makes vowel-like noises) or	Focuses on objects as well	• Loves looking at new faces. • Starting to smile

		babbles.	as adults.	• Smiles at parent
2.1–4.5 months	Rolls to the side using tummy. Rests on elbows, lifts head 90 degrees. Sits propped up with hands, head steady for short time.	Changes sounds while verbalizing, *"eee-ahhh"*. Verbalizes to engage someone in interaction. Blows bubbles, plays with tongue. Deep belly laughs.	Hand regard: following the hand with the eyes. Color vision adult-like.	Serves to practice emerging visual skills. Also observed in blind children.
3 months	Prone: head held	Makes	Follows	Squeals with

	up for prolonged periods. No grasp reflex.	vowel noises.	dangling toy from side to side. Turns head round to sound. Follows adults' gaze (joint attention). Sensitivity to binocular cues emerges.	delight appropriately. Discriminates smile. Smiles often. Laughs at simple things. Reaches out for objects.

5 months	Holds head steady. Goes for objects and gets them. Objects taken to mouth.	Enjoys vocal play.		Noticing colours. Adjusts hand shape to shape of toy before picking up.

6 months	Transfers objects from one hand to the other. Pulls self-up to sit and sits erect with supports. Rolls over prone to supine. Palmar grasp of cube hand to hand-eye coordination.	Double syllable sounds such as 'mumum' and 'dada'; babbles (consonant-vowel combinations).	Localizes sound 45 cm lateral to either ear. Visual acuity adult-like (20/20). Sensitivity to pictorial depth cues (those used by artists to indicate depth) emerges.	May show Stranger Anxiety.

9–10 months	Wiggles and crawls. Sits unsupported. Picks up objects with pincer grasp.	Babbles tunefully.	Looks for dropped toys.	Apprehensive about strangers.
1 year	Stands holding furniture. Stands alone for a second or two, then collapses with a bump.	Babbles 2 or 3 words repeatedly.	Drops toys, and watches where they go.	Cooperates with dressing Waves goodbye. Understands simple commands.
18 months	Can walk alone. Picks up toy without falling over. Gets up/down stairs holding onto rail. Begins to jump with both feet. Can build a tower	'Jargon'. Many intelligible words.	Be able to recognise their favourite songs, and will try to join in.	Demands constant mothering. Drinks from a cup with both hands. Feeds self with a spoon. Most children with

	of 3 or 4 cubes and throw a ball.			autism are diagnosed at this age.
2 years	Able to run. Walks up and down stairs 2 feet per step. Builds tower of 6 cubes.	Joins 2–3 words in sentences.		Parallel play. Dry by day.

3 years	Goes up stairs 1-foot per step and downstairs 2 feet per step. Copies circle, imitates hand motions and draws man on request. Builds tower of 9 cubes.	Constantly asks questions. Speaks in sentences.		Cooperative play. Undresses with assistance. Imaginary companions.
4 years	Goes down stairs one foot per step, skips on one foot. Imitates gate with cubes, copies a cross.	Questioning at its height. Many infantile substitutions in speech		Dresses and undresses with assistance. Attends to own toilet needs.

5 years	Skips on both feet and hops. Draws a man and copies a hexagonal based pyramid using graphing paper. Gives age.	Fluent speech with few infantile substitutions in speech.		Dresses and undresses alone.
6 years	Copies a diamond. Knows right from left and number of fingers.	Fluent speech.		

Chapter 3
Stages Of Child Development

Children go through a series of developmental stages as they grow up from being infants to teenagers to becoming adults. Though many parents might prioritize one stage over the other, it is important to know that each of these stages is crucial to the development of their child's individuality. Parents need to focus on their child's physical, emotional, intellectual, as well as social needs to help them grow into healthy individuals.

The role of the parent is not only to give encouragement to their child, but to also ensure that their child can take part in activities that will aid them to master crucial tasks of development. As a parent, you are the child's first teacher. It goes without saying that a parent should be their child's best teacher all through their life. As a parent, you should take some practical steps to help your child grow according to their age.

For example, a parent must expose their child to such challenges that are suitable to their age; this will help them develop in an age-appropriate manner. Then, a parent should make sure to allow their child such experiences, where they can go out and explore their surroundings independently. A child by interacting with their environment, can learn how to manoeuver their way around successfully.

According to Child Development specialists, children are motivated from the time of their birth to test their surroundings. It is through exploring and experimenting that they learn and develop. A parent's responsibility in this regard, is to give the required support to their child so that he or she may, in a safe and productive zone, discover and learn from the world around them. Every child has their own distinctive blueprint of development. A parent must keep this fact in mind, as they aid their child to grow.

Infants/Babies (0 – 2 years)

Raising an infant is a very challenging task, as any new parent will tell you. This stage is the time for the child to develop the bonds that will last him or her a lifetime. The bonds he or she forms will provide the child with the internal reserves that will help them develop their self-esteem. It will also allow them to advance their ability to relate to others positively and productively.

Again, parents must remember that a child is different with their unique personality and needs. It is essential for a parent to try and understand their child's personality. Also, a parent must encourage their child's distinctive characteristics and abilities, so that they can develop into healthy adults with a strong sense of self-confidence.

Toddlers/Preschoolers (2 – 5 years)

As a toddler or a preschooler, a child is able to move around freely and become acquainted with the world around them. Parents can regard this period of their child's life as a time for productive interaction with their environment. At this stage, a child's language ability grows by leaps and bounds. As a child learn the names of things around them, they also learn the skill of voicing their needs. They will ask for this or that object, or they will tell their parents they are hungry; for instance – something which they could not do before. Gradually, a child learns that he or she can be an independent individual; as a child does that, they also pick up the ability to refuse – that is, to say no.

At this stage of development, one of the primary tasks at hand is what psychologists term as emotional regulation. One ubiquitous occurrence that the parent of every child of this age witnesses is the 'meltdown.' A child at this stage will express him or herself without moderation. While this is pretty normal, parents can still work their way through the child's 'tantrums' by relying on the emotional link that their child has developed with them during their infancy.

Parents can guide their child gently to learn the skill of tempering their emotional expression. Parents will see their toddler say 'no' to things almost instinctively. However, parents have to teach their child to also accept refusal – or 'no' – from others around them. At this stage, parents also have to prepare their child to enter the school system. During this developmental stage, a child's intellectual skills develop along with his physical abilities. These developments take place at a fairly fast rate. A parent's role during this stage is to equip their child to interact amicably with the external world. At the same time, parents should teach their child to compete with their fellows; be it physically in games and sports, or intellectually in education.

A parent must become a coach to their child – someone who not only lays down the guidelines of contact with the world, but also gives the right amount of encouragement to reach out to others and form meaningful connections. Parents, to reiterate, are their child's first and best teacher. They continue to play a crucial role in helping their child form the necessary skills of communicating with others, experimenting with their environment and comprehension of new ideas and concepts.

School-Age Children (6 – 12 years)

For a parent, their child's time in school can give rise to very enriching experiences. Parents of children this age will watch their child try out new activities. They will cheer their kid on at sports competitions and will congratulate them on their academic achievements. The elements that a child experiences at this age are the highlights of the child's life for most of the parents. Notwithstanding that, it is also a fact that accomplishments go hand in hand with hitches and frustrations. A child at this age will experience triumphs but also failures.

So, the role of the parent at this stage is to prepare their child for both facets of life experiences. Parents should teach their child to acknowledge their weaknesses at the same time they celebrate their child's strengths and help them improve on those. Parents who are prepared to handle a child can be the best coach that the child needs to make sense of the world around them. Being a parent to an infant or toddler means being a constant supervisor to their activities. However, being a parent to a school-aged child means to allow their child freedom as an individual.

While children this age will want independence; they are in many ways, unequipped to handle themselves independently. In such instances, it becomes the responsibility of the parent to teach their child to make sound choices and take good decisions. Parents must help their child learn self-control and self-discipline. Parents should also instill a system of values in their child so that a child knows the difference between right and wrong, and is able to act according to that system.

It is usual for children this age to struggle with making important or even minor decisions. Thus, it is the parent's responsibility to step in and help their child work their way around things which might be too complicated for them. A parent should encourage their child to accomplish big things; at the same time, parents should allow their children to experience the results of their behaviour, if it transgresses against the code or the rules set in place. This is the only way for a child to grow by learning from their mistakes.

Adolescents/Teenagers (13 – 18 years)

Most parents would agree that their child's teenage is the most challenging time for them as parents. This is because a child starts to come into his or her own during the period of their adolescence. While this is an exciting time of self-discovery and growth for a child, it is also a period marked with several changes – these include hormonal, physical, intellectual and emotional changes.

While a teenager may experience such positive experiences, as independence and freedom to make decisions, they may also be exposed to negative acts such as that of peer pressure or bullying. In all, teenage remains a worrying time – both for the child as well as their parents.

As a child grows into a teenager, he or she might present such challenges as behaving in a passive-aggressive way; show self-consciousness, self-doubt and/or over-confidence; and of course, moodiness. Though this might appear scary to parents who mind find themselves unable to cope with the rapid changes in their child, rest assured that it is all very normal.

At this stage, a child undergoes puberty and experiences hormonal changes and rapid physical development. The edges of their personality become sharper; their character and selfhood fully emerge. A child this age looks to the future, as he or she deliberates over their goals in life. In the practical world, this development is mainly demonstrated through such acts of advanced aptitude as preparing for college, or going for a job or internship program. Teenagers also have several hobbies and innate talents, which they explore and improve during this time.

Then, another important aspect is the development of social skills. Teenagers form connections with people around them and develop meaningful relationships with their peers. As they contend with social pressures such as peer influence, they learn to form appropriate responses to the several temptations that they face on a daily basis. They learn to prioritize and go for what will benefit them as they are no longer merely instinctual beings, but logical ones.

Logically speaking, children need their parents at this stage, perhaps more so than ever before. Teenagers can experience a wholesome adolescent period, if their family environment is positive and encouraging.

They can form strong relationships with their parents and take part in community service, as well as in extracurricular activates. It is the parents' responsibility to help their child navigate their teenage years as smoothly as possible.

Chapter 4
Styles Of Parenting

The upbringing of a child is not as easy as it sounds. It requires various strategies and the psychological construct of those strategies is what makes up different parenting styles. The categorization of specific behaviors based on parental practices are represented through these patterns, labeled as parenting styles. Various researches have proven that children who are found to be more competent in being socially skilled and proficient, are the ones who are independent.

The competency is also subject to the firm control parents have over their children, giving them independence at the same time. Researches have been conducted as early as the mid-80s which focus on how different parenting styles have various impacts. The list of researches includes the research by Diana Baumrind, an American developmental psychologist. In her research, she studied how parenting styles impact on child upbringing and identified four styles of parenting. The kind of parenting style you choose, which could affect your parental skills positively or negatively is extremely important.

Authoritative Parenting

The description of this style of parenting can be described as demanding and responsive. This child-centered approach holds maturity expectations. Parents who are authoritative know how their children feel and based on that understanding, guide their children to regulate their feelings. Forgiveness is the key. Despite having high maturity expectations, the possible shortcomings are ignored and forgiven.

In fact, parents help their children find solutions to the problems they encounter in this style. Independence is often misunderstood by having no limitations, but this definitely is not the case. Authoritative parents have limitations set for their child. When parents are warm and nurturing, they do not refuse the substantial verbal give and take, but rather allow the child to be free to explore.

This greatly improves their decision-making capability, which is based on their own understanding. Children of authoritative parents are self-reliant. Usually, high parental demands lead to authoritative parenting style. The standards that authoritative parents set, which monitor the limits and development of autonomy, raise their level of satisfaction while testing the maturity and assessing general behavior. Children are punished on misbehaving but those punishments are not violent.

Often it isn't the punishment but the hypothetical understanding of the consequences, which follow the child's actions, is discussed to help the child understand the inappropriate behavior in order to prevent from repeating. Authoritative parents can be demanding when it comes to the maturity they expect from their child. Also, they set limitations and try to ensure that those are taken seriously.

They also tend to give encouragement wherever necessary. However, when a child is punished, there will be a reason validating their punishment. As authoritative parenting has fair punishments, children are more responsive. Another reason why the children of authoritative parents are more likely to be successful is that they become self-determined, as well as generous.

Authoritarian Parenting

The authoritarian parenting style is a restrictive one. It involves heavy punishments, which reflects the focus of the parents on status and family perception, without any regard for attaining any constructive feedback from the child in most cases. To enforce discipline, shouting and spanking are the frequently employed tools. The purpose is to make the child behave like an adult in a society that can be unforgiving.

In this way, they attempt to prepare their child for the negative aggressive reactions faced by them, if the standard norms are not followed. Parents following this parental style have a belief system that eases dealing with stress, whether it is acute or chronic. The effects of authoritative parenting are peculiar to children. The lack of social competence in children being treated under such a parenting style occurs, because children are always told what they are supposed to do.

They are not allowed to make their own choices. This might help to improve results on a short-term basis; but in the long run, there is a decline in the child's development when it comes to identifying opportunities and taking command. These children are well-accustomed to conformity, obedience and self-blame. This may also lead them to depression as their understanding of happiness also gets tampered and complex.

In some cases, the child's behavior does not change even when they enter adulthood. Children raised through the authoritarian parenting style develop self-confidence at an early age. On entering adolescence, they might even get rebellious. When a high self-blame level is combined with a lack of confidence, the behavior of children gets transformed into an escapist one.

The risks of suicide and drug abuse increase greatly. Authoritative parenting is usually a part of the culture of different societies across the globe. These societies are mostly inhabited in African regions, where child-rearing customs are commonly practiced. It wouldn't be wrong to say that most parents practicing the authoritative parenting style have some aspect of it integrated into their ethnicity.

Indulgent Or Permissive Parenting

To be responsive and yet not demanding, are the traits of this parenting style. Libertarian, Permissive or Indulgent parenting is characterized to have minimum expectations with respect to the behavior of the child. The parenting style of highly involved parents is known as the indulging parenting style. Here, the parents start demanding, while controlling their children's lives to a considerable extent.

Parents become highly responsive to their children's needs and desires without any requirements of appropriate behavior. When children are accustomed to little or no aggression even when behaving inappropriately, it could hit them as a surprise. Not knowing how others react when they behave inappropriately, they pay less attention to their behavior, which results in them not having a decent behavior themselves.

Permissive parents seek the friendship of their children. They apparently do not focus on acting as a parent. As a result, the expectations of these children are very low with regards to parenting discipline. Such parents give their children friendly advice and are allowed total control over their decision-making process.

This is a very relaxed parenting style where the concept of punishment is close to being non-existent. The wants along with the needs of the children are fulfilled. Permissive parents tend to provide their children with freedom and materials they did not have in their own childhood, as compensation for what they missed themselves.

According to Baurmind's research, children of permissive parents were found to be immature. They lacked impulsive control, therefore, making them irresponsible. At an adolescent age, children of such parents may be more engaged in misconduct, thus being more impulsive. These children are unable to control their own behavior and become overly dominant.

They accept their defeat willingly as they are emotionally secure. They also learn to live by themselves as children of permissive parents are independent and mature sooner than children of parents having other parenting styles. From a recent study, parents who were successful in practicing accountability had children who were least prone to heavy drinking when they got in their teenage. These parents were high on warmth.

The so-called 'indulgent' parents, were found to be low on accountability, having children highly prone to heavy drinking. These parents were also considered to be high on warmth. 'Strict parents' or authoritarian parents also had high risks of their children being prone to drinking when entering adulthood. These parents are considered to be high on accountability and low in warmth.

Neglectful Or Uninvolved Parenting

Neglectful parenting is uninvolved and dismissive. The parents are extremely low in both warmth and control. Neglectful parents are least involved in their children's lives being disengaged and undemanding. Since they do not pay much attention to their children, they set no limits and neither are they actively responsible. In extreme cases, these parents have no regard for their children's emotions or opinions. Their children lack emotional support as a result, and only have their basic needs fulfilled; i.e., things required for them to stay alive such as food and healthcare. There can be various causes that lead to neglectful parenting style.

This may include parent's self-prioritization, financial issues or drug addiction. This parenting style usually leads to lack of encouragement and even communication, therefore, drawing the child away from his/her parents. Children consider their lives to be less important when compared to their parents. Such children start believing themselves to have matured beyond their age.

As a result, they try providing for themselves. Parents and children often display contradictory behavior. It becomes difficult for them to come to an agreement, as the parent acts demanding and authoritative while the child remains resentful. Also, the probability of children developing social anxiety disorder is high. This disturbed attachment may also influence their relationship throughout their lives. Patterns of absenteeism and delinquency are prominent in adolescence in affected children. Young individuals raised through this parenting style lack an internal sense of discipline. Since the children lack expression of love, they try to get it from whatever sources they can.

The study conducted by Maccoby and Martin in 1983 analyzed adolescents between the ages of 14–18 years in four areas: psychosocial development (evaluating mental growth), school achievement (getting accustomed to rewards), internalized distress (dealing with self-issues) and problem behavior. The tests of the study resulted in neglectful parents scoring the lowest, while authoritative parents scoring the highest.

It is important for parents to consider these parenting styles but work towards Authoritative Parenting. This style of parenting uses both nurture and structure, which allows you as a parent to manage challenging behaviors in a positive way. Being an authoritative parent enables you to be effective, consistent, and firm; and above all, a loving parent at all stages. This indicates that this style of parenting has the most successful outcomes for child development.

Chapter 5
Disciplining Your Child

"When a child hits a child, we call it aggression. When a child hits an adult, we call it hostility. When an adult hits an adult we call it assault but when an adult hits a child, we call it discipline".

-Haim Ginott

It is important that as a parent, discipline should be a tool you must use in the upbringing of your child. Comprehensively, discipline is training and enforcing people to follow a code of conduct and abide by the rules, whatever they might be. Punishments are used to correct disobedience and ensure consistent behavior.

Many parents are quick to correlate Physical Chastisement to discipline. Some parents grew up in environments where physical chastisement is a form of discipline and good home training; and this is a paramount belief in the upbringing of children. In some religions – *"spare the rod, spoil the child"* proverb has embedded into the belief system that this is a way of getting children to be respectful, courteous and behave appropriately in the society. Many Africans and Asians understand discipline to be physical chastisement and violence to correct behavior. They believe that the Western culture of *"reasonable chastisement"* means children are being brought up with no respect for authority.

Some parents have expressed fear and worry that the lack of physical chastisement will lead their children to be disrespectful and wayward. It is possible to bring up well-adjusted and disciplined children without the use of force, violence, or aggression. There are appropriate ways of disciplining your child in stages as stated below:

Discipline In Stages
Ages 0 To 2

Babies and toddlers are naturally curious. Therefore, it is wise to eliminate temptations — items such as TVs, other video equipment, stereos, jewelry, and especially cleaning supplies and medicines should be kept well out of their reach. It is obvious that a crawling baby has no sense of anything around him. It is learning about cold and hot sensations and experimenting with everything around him. When you find your child moving towards a dangerous object just calmly say 'No'. At times it works, mostly it doesn't. The smarter thing to do then is to distract them and remove them the area of danger.

Also, timeouts can serve effectively. Any child who has been misbehaving like hitting or throwing away objects particularly food need to be told why the behavior is not acceptable. This is done by taking them to a time-out area, designated for this purpose. The timeout should not be long; as longer timeouts are not at all effective for children younger than two years. The purpose is to calm them down and make them understand that they are at fault.

Often overlooked, the behavior of hitting has a solid impact on a child of any age and the impact is never a good one. It is extremely important not to hit a child under any circumstances. Whether it be slapping or spanking, it is only going to make the situation worse. Babies are very young to relate the physical punishment to their behavior and when they are hit, the pain they feel overrides any other emotion of behavior realization.

In addition, do not forget that children learn by watching adults, particularly their parents. Make sure your behavior provides a role-model. You will be better understood if you start of by taking care of your belongings and putting them away, rather than just telling your toddler to do so.

Ages 3 to 5

As children grow and begin to establish a connection between their actions and its consequences, it is essential for you to communicate with them the rules of your family and home. Children need to know what your expectations are, before they are punished for any particular behavior.

Almost every three-year-old picks up pencils or crayons, and starts displaying his skill on the walls of your house. You need to discuss it with him about why it isn't allowed, and you need to tell him about the consequences if he or she does it again. The consequences can include not allowing them to use crayons for the entire day or even having to clean the affected wall. If the wall is yet again decorated, first remind them that crayons are to be used on paper and if they still fail to understand, it's about time you enforce the communicated consequences. The sooner parents establish the tone that they are the ones who are going to be making the rules and the children are to follow them, the easier it is to groom them with discipline.

It is often easier for parents to ignore occasional bad behavior, which includes not enforcing the consequences. However, this behavior sets a bad precedent. If you aren't consistent, you cannot be good at giving discipline. This is why parents should decide together what the home rules should include, and then they must uphold them with fervor.

Obviously, single parents do not perform much consultation, as they are responsible individually for all the important decisions. While you become clear on what behavior will be punished, do not forget to reward good behavior. Your 'praise' has a positive effect; do not underestimate it as discipline is not a synonym for punishment, and acknowledging good behavior is also a key part of it. Saying *"I'm proud you shared your lunch box"* is usually way more effective than punishing a child who did not share. Moreover, be specific when giving praise rather than just saying *"Good job!"* If your child continues an unacceptable behavior despite your efforts, it's about time you make a chart that has a box for each day. You need to decide how many times your child can misbehave before he needs to be punished.

Similarly, the chart will also include the time duration of practicing proper behavior required to be rewarded. Stick the chart on the refrigerator or somewhere easily visible to both you and your child. This will help you track the day-to-day behavior of the kid. Both parties will know about the current behavior situation. Once it starts to work, keep motivating and praising your child on showing good behavior. Timeouts also work well for children this age. Pick a suitable timeout place that has no distractions.

The reason behind choosing such a place is because the child will have time to think about how he or she has behaved. Often parents send children to their rooms where they have television sets or computers. This kills the purpose of corrective detention. If you don't get the child in an environment where he gets time to think about how he behaved wrong, he might never think about it and the behavior will not be rectified.

Be certain about the time duration that would be best for your child. According to experts, a minute for each year of age is a good enough rule of thumb, while others suggest that the timeout should be continued unless the child calms down to help the child learn self-regulation.

It is important to tell children about the right way of doing things, rather than just telling them what they have done wrong. For instance, rather than scolding kids who jump on the bed, tell them politely that the bed is used only for resting.

Ages 6 to 8

Timeouts are the most effective discipline strategy for this age group. This is the age in which implying consistency is the most difficult yet the most required practice. If you tell such children about the consequences but do not enforce them when the time comes, you undermine your own authority. Children must believe that you mean what you say.

This is not to say that your children cannot have any second chances. There is always a margin of error with children, but more often than not your action and speech should be on the same page. The problem arises when parents make unrealistic threats in anger, which are hard for them to follow through. Avoid doing this mistake.

If you threaten to go back home, if your child does not stop whining to the count of three, make sure you do. The credibility you will gain with your children is way more valuable than the fun and excitement you might miss by canceling the plans and going back home. Also, prolonged punishments might take away the power and respect you are entitled to, as a parent.

If the punishment is for a long period of time, it might kill away the motivation to change behavior, as everything may already be taken away; for instance, if the child is grounded for a month.

Ages 9 to 12

Children of this age group demand independence and responsibility. Like all other age groups, they are better disciplined by facing natural consequences. This is an effective and appropriate method for implementing discipline. For example, if your fifth grader's homework has not been done on time you do not have to worry about it and perform an intervention.

If you do make them stay up late or help them finish their homework, you might take from them the opportunity to learn a key life lesson. When the child will go to school with incomplete homework, it will affect his grade and he or she will understand that it's their responsibility and no one else. Every parent wants to rescue their children from making mistakes, but sometimes they do their children a favor by letting them fail.

In this manner, children learn themselves what behaving improperly can do to them and they avoid making such mistakes in the future. However, if the natural consequences fail to teach them any life lessons, you need to fabricate a few for them, as it is important that they learn them at the right time.

Ages 13 and Up

At this stage, you have already laid the groundwork. Your child knows what is expected and you mean what you say about the penalties for bad behavior. Do not let your guard down now — discipline is just as important for teenagers as it is for younger children. Teenagers need defined boundaries more than people of any age group. You need to set up rules for almost everything.

They may include policies for homework, curfews,

dating and even seeing friends. There have to be limitations for every activity. It is wiser to discuss with your child beforehand, in order to avoid any misunderstanding. Your teenager will probably complain from time to time, but will also realize that you are in control.

Believe it or not, teenagers require you to set limits for them. You are the one who has to enforce order in their lives, even as their freedom and responsibilities increase. When your teenager breaks a rule, taking away their privileges might seem the best course of action. While it is fine to take away the car for a week; for example, be sure to discuss why coming home an hour past curfew is unacceptable and worrisome. Remember to give your teen control to some extent.

This will make your teen respect the decisions you make, while limiting the number of power struggles you may encounter. You may allow a younger teen to make decisions concerning school clothes or hairstyles. As the teen grows older, control has to be extended which might include a relaxed curfew occasionally. Focusing on the positives is essential. For example, your teen could earn a later curfew by demonstrating positive behavior or vice versa.

A Word About Spanking

Spanking is a very controversial form of discipline. There are reasons why experts discourage spanking:

- Spanking teaches children that it is ' OK' to hit when they experience anger.

- Children can be physically harmed through spanking.

- Spanking does not teach children about how they are to change their behavior but rather makes them fearful of their parents.

- It teaches them to avoid being caught instead of rectifying their mistakes.

- For children seeking attention by acting out, spanking inadvertently *"rewards"* them — negative attention is better than no attention at all.

Chapter 6
Childhood Difficulties

Recognizing childhood difficulties is essential in the upbringing of children. Most parents fail to recognize these difficulties, which then causes hurdles and produces frustration for both, parent and child. Some of these difficulties can be frustrating and daunting. However, it can be handled easily when these difficulties are observed and handled effectively.

There is a likelihood that some children may be unable to exhibit characteristics within their age range. Some children may experience behavioral problems and feelings. Some may experience mental health difficulties and physical disabilities. It is important that parents seek appropriate medical help, as soon as possible, when they observe that something is not right. Being a parent, it is important to be observant on these challenges and difficulties to avoid aggravating the situation.

Some childhood difficulties include:

ADHD – Attention Deficit Hyperactive Disorder

ADD – Attention Deficit Disorder

ASD – Autism Spectrum Disorder

OCD – Obsessive Compulsive Disorder

PD – Psychotic Disorder

LD – Learning Disability

Learning Disability

The most challenging childhood difficulty a lot of parents struggle with is managing children with Learning Disability. The Royal College of Psychiatrists has a complete case study which conclusively states that it is more difficult for a child with the general learning disability to learn and perform tasks, as compared to the other children of the same age.

Children with learning disabilities gradually learn throughout their childhood. For them, it is a slow step by step process where they understand things at their own pace. The degree of disability can vary. Some disabilities are severe in which children never learn to speak. They might even require help for looking after themselves. For tasks like feeding, dressing and visiting the bathroom, they need assistance and are unable to do it on their own.

In some cases, the disability can be mild where the child grows up to become an independent individual and has the capability to look after his/her self. The causes of this disability may include genetic factors or could be a result of an infection, brain injury, and damage at birth or after it.

Down's syndrome, cerebral palsy and Fragile X syndrome are all its examples. Learning disability in children has a great impact on the entire family. It is important that as a parent you are adequately informed and aware of these disabilities. It's not that children or young people having general learning disability are unaware of what is happening around them, but their ability to express and communicate is limited in most cases.

Additionally, speech problems make it even more difficult for them to explain their feelings and needs. This makes them feel frustrated by their own limitations. They only feel sad and angry when they compare themselves to other children. They fall into a state where they wage a war against themselves. Parents of children with general learning disability have to be very strong, as the fact of having an affected child itself can be very distressing.

It can be hard to swallow the news and then explain it to other members of the family about the condition of their child. It is not easy to manage their child's behavior and it seems as though nobody else understands. The siblings of such a child may also be affected. Since a child with the disability requires more attention, their siblings might feel jealous. They may also feel embarrassed by their disabled sibling's behavior.

They may even be teased at school and end up hating their sibling for being the reason behind teasing. Often they believe that they are responsible for their distressed parents and disabled sibling. Being a parent, recognizing that a child with general learning disability learns at a slow pace is very important. When the problem is recognized on time, support and help can be offered. Disability does not mean the child cannot have an enjoyable life. The child deserves an enjoyable life just as the rest of the kids do. The mission of all specialist organizations is to help such children, who have a general learning disability to lead lives that are as fulfilling as those of anyone else. It is important that parents seek medical attention when they experience these challenges in their children.

Chapter 7

Effective Key Steps To Raising Children

It is important that as parents, our values and beliefs are passed on to our children in a positive environment. Raising children is a tough yet fulfilling job. You might also feel that you are the least prepared for it. Here are some key tips that may ease the process of parenting for you, and more importantly allow your child to receive parenting in the best way.

Step 1

- Boosting and Building Your Child's Self-Esteem and mental well-being

Building and boosting your child's mental well-being is very important. Children see their own selves as babies when they look at themselves through their parents' eyes. They absorb your tone of voice, body language, and every expression. Being a parent, your actions and speech have a direct impact on the development of their self-esteem more than anything else in their environment. As a parent, you should avoid using words as a weapon. The damage caused by negative comments is not indifferent to physical blows. Statements like *"What a stupid thing to do!"* or *"I wish you were as smart as your younger brother"* may vandalize their personality.

Try not to be too critical of their behavior. Focus on the issues and not their personality. Insults, curses and harsh words are the easiest and fastest ways of breaking them down and destroying their self-confidence. Comparison with other children or siblings should be a 'no no'! It makes children feel worthless and diverts their attention toward unproductive competition that has the potential to create complexities in their approach towards life at a young age.

Choosing your words carefully and being compassionate in your speech makes children think that everybody is entitled to make mistakes. And that your love has no proportionality to the right or wrong they do, even when you do not love their behavior. Encourage children to be independent and be themselves. In doing so, be clear about acceptable and unacceptable behaviors. Allowing children to participate is important to polish their decision-making skills. Let them be a part of setting rules and regulations in the home. This way, it shows that you value their intellect and want to use their input. When strong bonding is developed with your children, they let you indulge in their lives and activities to the extent that you want as a parent.

This lets you find out when something is right or wrong without them being present. Spending time each day to talk to your child is very important. Explore their experiences for the day, discuss any challenges they might have faced, and motivate them as much as possible. You build their confidence and trust this way.

It is important to attend school activities involving your child. This practice allows you to show that you are concerned about their education and activities at school. Use the reward system model. A hug, a kiss, or a hi-five will go a long way in maintaining the mental well-being of your child.

Step 2

- Catch Children Being Good

An effective approach is to catch children doing something right such as, *"You cleaned your room without being asked — good job!"* or *"I was watching you share with your sister and you were very kind, great job or well done!"* Instead of repeated scolding, such statements can be used to encourage good behavior considerably.

It's simple, find something to praise them every day. Even praise the small accomplishments as they would make them feel proud. This would encourage them to do things on their own in an independent fashion, giving them a sense of capability and strength.

There has to be generosity while you give rewards; be it a physical display of love or verbal appreciation. Soon you would notice your child behaving appropriately, just like you would have wanted them to.

Step 3

- Consistency in your Discipline and Set Limits

Discipline is essential for every child. It enforces self-control, making the child distinguish and opt for appropriate behavior. Children will always test their limits. It is a natural behavior, but remember the purpose of setting those limits is to help them grow into responsible adults. When house rules are established, it helps children interpret your expectations, helping them develop self-control.

Some rules can include not using the smartphone until homework is done or not allowing hitting other children. An organized system could be the solution, such as a couple of warnings followed by penalization or loss of prerogatives.

Inconsistency is a common mistake made by parents – which is the failure to follow through with the consequences. It would definitely not be wise to punish your child for indiscipline one day and ignoring it the next. If you won't be consistent, the child won't know what you expect from them.

Step 4

- Create quality time for Your Children

It is sometimes difficult for parents and children to get together for family meals, or spend quality time together. However, there is probably nothing more that children would like than to spend time with their parents. For instance, getting up 10 minutes earlier in the morning to have breakfast with your child or involving them in domestic activities like cleaning the house together can be productive.

When children are not paid the required amount of attention, they misbehave as they get find it is a good way to get noticed by their parents. Many parents sit with their children and plan out spending time together each week. It could be a 'special night' or a regular dinner. Children can even suggest ways in which they can spend quality time with their parents.

Adolescents do not require undivided attention, as

much as the younger ones do. The window of opportunity for parents and teenagers to spend time together is very narrow with busy lifestyles. It is important to somehow manage and be available, when teenagers want to communicate or get involved in family activities. Playing games or attending concerts with your teen might help you understand your child better and know more about the friends they have. Do not feel guilty if you work and stay busy. Children remember the little things that you should provide.

Step 5

- Build parental integrity – A Good Role Model by example

Young children observe how their parents act and attempt to mirror it. The younger the child, the more observant he/she is of you, following you more than the siblings. Before you lose it in front of your child, just remind yourself that this is not how you want your children to behave. Your children are constantly watching you. Various studies show that most children hit others, because of the aggressive role model they have at home, which is either of their parents.

You have to model the traits you wish your children to have: respect, friendliness, honesty, kindness, and tolerance. Exhibit unselfish behavior. When you do things without the greed of being rewarded and offer compliments, your child does the same. And most importantly, treat your children the way you would want to be treated.

Step 6

- Make Communication a number one Priority

You cannot expect children to do everything simply because you, as a parent, want them to. Just like how adults want explanations so do children. If we do not explain, children start questioning the motives and values taught by us to them, and wonder if all our teachings are baseless. Explanations allow your child to understand and learn in a non-judgmental manner.

Make your expectations clear to them. Problems will always exist. It would only be smart to discuss them with your child. Do not hold yourself from expressing what you feel and communicate with your child for solutions. Clearly tell them about the possible consequences of their actions. Do not give an order but offer choices and be open to suggestions yourself. Be the negotiator as children who participate in decisions have a higher level of motivation to follow them through.

Step 7

- Be Flexible and Willing to Adjust Your Parenting Style

Your parenting style should be dynamic. It has to evolve just like the growth of your child. Chances are that what works with your child now might not work a year later. Their role models change with age. You might have been a role model when they were young but when they enter teenage, their peers are more likely to inspire them.

Guidance and encouragement are essential for your

child's growth. But there has to be a balance that comes with disciplined independence. These combinations greatly enhance positive child behavior. In addition, there should be moments where you sense a connection with your child and establish a bond with them.

Step 8

- Show Unconditional Love

It is your duty as a parent to correct and guide your children. Your expression of corrective guidance plays a critical role in how it is to be perceived by the child. Avoid blaming or criticizing your children when confronting them. It could undermine their self-esteem, leading to resentment. Even when disciplining them, you need to encourage them towards positive behavior. They should know that your love will always be there, even if they do not meet your expectations.

Step 9

- Create and build your child's physical security

Creating and building your child's physical security is paramount as an effective parent. When a child makes a disclosure or reports about abuse or a situation involving bullying, it is imperative as a parent to deal with it as soon as possible. When children are confident and assured of physical security from their parents, it goes a long way to reassure them that they are secured and safe in all their activities.

It is also important that you avoid being angry when instilling discipline in your child. It sends a negative signal to them. Take time to calm down before taking any disciplinary action. If someone else has made you upset, do not take it out on your child. If the child has made you upset, calm down.

If punishment is necessary when the child misbehaves, removal of privileges, time-out and consequential situations work better than smacking, scolding, or the use of harsh words. If you offend your child when in anger, apologize immediately. Apology sends a positive signal and reassures the children that they are human and your love is paramount to the offense.

Step 10

- Acknowledge Your Own Needs and Limitations as a Parent

If you have your own needs and limitations as a parent, acknowledge them. You are not a perfect parent; nobody is. There are strengths and weaknesses associated with you as a family leader. You need to recognize your abilities and work on your weaknesses.

You cannot have all the answers. Have realistic expectations from yourself, your spouse and most importantly, your children. Learn to be forgiving to yourself. In addition, concentrate your focus on areas that need the most attention, instead of attempting to address everything at once. Parenting is a managerial job; manage it.

There is no harm in admitting when you are tired and burned out. Take time out for yourself. Get involved in things that give you pleasure as a person or a couple. It isn't wrong to care about your own well-being and it is another important value to model for your children.

Yes, it is important that you enhance yourself as a parent in different ways. For example, learn more on parenting by attending parenting classes or seminars, read books on parenting or motivational topics, attend social events, have a positive orientation about life, about yourself, your spouse and your children. If you seem to be falling short in some of these areas, seek help where available.

You are a Parent	You are Powerful	You are Strong
P – Positioned To	**P** – Passionately	**S** – Standing
A – Adequately	**O** – Optimistic	**T** – Together
R – Raise	**W** – Wise	**R** – Raising
E – Educate	**E** – Encouraging	**O** – Our
N – Nurture	**R** – Resilient	**N** – Next
T – Train	**F** – Faithful	**G** –Generation
	U – Unified	
	L – Leader	

Chapter 8

Importance Of Parenting Classes, Seminars And Conferences

Parenting definitely does not come with a manual on how to do everything from birth to adulthood. While all children develop at different rates, a parenting seminar can give you a time frame as to when these milestones should occur -- and let you know when you should consult with your pediatrician if your child is not reaching a milestone. Such a seminar will generally discuss other issues and problems that parents face.

Sometimes parents do not realize that the parenting style they use will harm their children more than helping them. When you enroll in parenting seminars, you learn new techniques, but before you can begin implementing what you learn in parenting seminars, you must work on identifying and understanding your own issues.

Parenting classes, seminars or conferences offer an efficient platform to support parents and caregivers of children. They focus on engagement, advocacy and training towards attaining skills needed for self-empowerment.

The activities within these events are aimed towards helping parents who are struggling in parenting. These platforms allow parents to retrospect on what they have been used to and let them acquire new skills in helping them become better parents.

Socialization

Parenting seminars allow you to make new friends who are dealing with similar issues. Furthermore, your new friends will likely have children the same age, so you can set up play dates, giving your child a chance to socialize with others. Parenting seminars are also a good way to obtain recommendations for pediatricians, child psychologists, nutritionists and educationists. Once the seminars are over, you'll find that these friends are valuable, especially when you want another parent's

opinion on a problem you're facing or need suggestions to
make a parenting choice

Chapter 9

Parents Heal Thyself

Why it is important for parents to identify their own issues? Many parents realize that they could benefit by learning different parenting techniques through parenting seminars and engaging with parental mentors. This can help you understand your children better, and know that you are not alone in the challenges you face as a parent.

The single most effective thing you can do is explore your own upbringing and identify issues you may have. Until you identify and work through issues in your own life, you will have problems implementing what you learn as a parent.

Parenting seminars encourage participants to explore their own issues and work on any that the attendees may have. It is common for adults to suffer from various issues and not even know it. These seminars can help parents understand their children.

Parenting Choices

As a parent, it's not uncommon to sometimes ask yourself, *"Am I doing this right?"* Parenting seminars can also discuss parenting skills, offering advice on how to handle problems that arise - from tantrums in little ones to defiant behavior in older children. You can get the affirmation you need that you are making appropriate decisions regarding your child -- and talk with other parents facing the same issues. You might discover that there are other ways to address problems, as well as other methods for disciplining your child or dealing with parent/child power struggles. You might leave a seminar with a new perspective on your parenting choices. This way, you become an Effective Parent with a practical understanding of successful child upbringing.

Chapter 10

Conclusion
Top Ten Tips for Parents
How to be the Best Parent

Parenting is the most important job that any of us can ever have: raising children to become responsible, caring, compassionate, and resilient can be a daunting task. It is also one of the most challenging and frustrating. However, parents need and deserve support and information to help them do the best they can in this critical task.

- There are no perfect parents – mistakes are chances to learn.

- Take care of yourself so you have energy to care for your children.

- Do not live through your children – meet your needs through your own efforts.

- Support and give your children the skills to solve their own problems – avoid being a *"helicopter"* parent.

- You have many years to raise your children – focus on one or two concerns at a time.

- Pick and choose from your upbringing how you want to parent.

- Create family traditions to pass on memories and values.

- *"Get on the same page"* for larger parenting decisions with those who share in your children's care.

- Seek support when you need it.

- Maintain a sense of humour.

Parents and their children are better off when moms and dads:

- take care of themselves,

- give themselves credit for all the good things they are doing,

- have people in their lives who will offer them support and appreciation for their efforts.

Parenting Tips for raising children.

- Create a respectful, loving home.

- Listen to your children's feelings and thoughts.

- Focus on the positives in your children.

- Allow your children to do things for themselves so they feel competent.

- Have realistic expectations – learn about child development.

- Hold children accountable by setting rules and following through on consequences. Do not hit, blame, or shame.

- Expect mistakes (yours and theirs). Use them as learning opportunities.

- Behave how you want your children to behave.

- Maintain a sense of humour.

- Know your values – use them to raise kids you like and respect.

When raising children, it is important to think about your long-term goals for them — what qualities, values, traits do you want them to have as adults? If you don't know where you are going, you are less likely to get there. It comes down to having a loving connection in which your children are willing to follow your guidance. Being an effective parent includes not only loving your children, but also disciplining them so they learn how to behave and become capable and caring adults.

There is no *"one size fits all"* approach to parenting, and everyone needs to find what works best for him and his particular child. However, these broad Top Ten Tips offer a foundation upon which you can create a supportive and optimistic attitude in your family.

What Communication Skills Should I Use with My Child?

Here are the **Top 10 Communication Tips** to learn how to talk to your children and have them listen to you:

- Listen without judgment.

- Accept feelings; limit unacceptable behaviour.

- Look for underlying feelings and unmet needs.

- Communicate your feelings without blaming or shaming.

- Stay calm in the heat of the moment.

- Use praise: Catch them being good.

- Encourage children to stick with challenging tasks.

- Hold family meetings to let everyone have a say.

- Correct without criticizing.

- Use humour to ease tension.

Learning when to listen and when to talk OR when to teach and when to let your children figure out their own solutions can help build a stronger relationship between you. There are wide ranges of healthy responses and rarely is there just one *"right"* way to react. By filling your tool belt with all of the communication skills, you will know how to use each one and when you want to reach for it.

Having these skills can assist you throughout your everyday interactions with your children and during those more difficult talks – such as about sex, trauma, death, or other emotionally charged situations.

How do I Discipline my Child?

Here are the **Top 10 Tips** for discipline:

- Be the leader in your home.

- Use discipline to teach and not to punish.

- Remain calm; you can fake it.

- Establish clear rules.

- Set expectations based on child's abilities.

- Follow through on consequences.

- Be flexible; but don't *"cave"* because you fear a fight.

- Get on the same page with your co-parent.

- Brainstorm with your kids to solve problems.

- Build a loving relationship so your kids will follow your guidance.

When you discipline your child, you can think to yourself, *"What does he need to learn in this situation to grow and mature?"* For example, does he need to learn to use his words instead of acting out, to control his impulses, or how to calm himself down?
Children need their parents to provide love. They also need their parents to:

- guide them,

- hold them accountable,

- help them gain the skills they will need to function in the world.

By providing structure, you are aiding your children in developing inner discipline to become responsible adults.

There is no one *"right"* way to set limits. There are wide ranges of healthy discipline approaches. Parents need to avoid the extremes of being overly lax and neglectful without providing sufficient guidance *or* being overly rigid and strict. Using harsh discipline that does not respect the child.

How Do I Manage Anger – Mine and My Children's?

Parents and children: do not blow your tops.

Here are the **Top 10 Tips** to manage anger –

- Accept anger as a normal emotion.

- Don't respond to your children's anger with outbursts of your own.

- Let your kids know when and why you are angry. This can improve your relationship.

- Think about anger triggers – feelings not heard or needs not met.

- Know signs of growing anger – sweaty palms,

heart beating fast, clenching teeth, stomach-ache.

- Listen to your children's angry feelings.

- Teach children to *"use their words"* rather than act out their feelings.

- Show children ways to calm down – doing jumping jacks, counting to ten, blowing bubbles, taking deep breaths.

- Show your anger in ways that do not blame or shame.

- Be patient – managing anger is the work of a lifetime.

The heat of the moment is not the best time to teach children. When strong emotions are present, parents may over-react. Children may not be able to use the thinking part of their brains. The best time to teach children how to behave is when everyone is calm.

Emotions come and go. On average, emotions pass in 90 seconds. By waiting, you have a better chance of sharing your feelings in a healthy way.

What are the Best Ways for Raising Teenagers?

As teens move toward greater independence, they often rebel and resist parental rules. This requires parents to adjust some of their tried-and-true approaches that may have been effective when their children were younger. Changing some rules and giving more privileges as teens show better judgment are ways you can help them to slowly gain maturity.

Parents do best if they do not take their teens' actions as personal assaults on them, but rather if they think their children are *"just doing their job"* of growing up. Teens are rapidly changing and often their lives are filled with emotional, physical, intellectual, and social turmoil. Understanding this helps parents manage their child's new and rocky stage of development.

Here are the **Top 10 Tips** for raising teenagers:

- Respect and listen to them.

- Reward increasing maturity with more freedom.

- Take away privileges if they can't handle the

freedom.

- Set clear and firm rules.

- Hold them accountable – set and follow through with consequences.

- Expect them to keep their word and you do the same.

- Do not take difficult behaviours as a dare or challenge.

- Accept that peers are an important influence.

- Know that teens need you in their lives, but on their terms.

- Continue to share your values.

Remember that teens can be passionate, exuberant, fun, idealistic, and creative. Raising them can fill your life with the same.

The End

EFFECTIVE PARENTING INITIAITVE PROJECT

Effective Parenting Initiative – providing parental education and child protection support services for families

This project provides early intervention programmes in reducing the number of children subject to child protection services or the removal of children from their families and placed in the care system. The aim and objective is to provide positive parenting skills to parents and caregivers in the community.

- *About New Era Initiative*

Established in April 2013, New Era Initiative is a charity and its foundation is based on community cohesion and development. New Era Initiative has developed a widely accepted project – Effective Parenting Initiative in Liverpool, United Kingdom by bringing specialist knowledge and expertise in parenting.

- *What we do*

NEI works is five key areas to help deliver early invention services in promoting the wellbeing of families and children living in the UK.

Our Key Work Areas:

- Parental Education

- Awareness Raising on Children's Rights

- Policy and Advocacy

- Education, Research and Advisory Services

- Community Development

- Support for young people and families in crisis

- ***Parental Education***

We offer positive Parental Education to parents and caregivers as an early intervention and prevention service in reducing the number of children taken into the care system.

- ***Awareness Raising on Children's Rights***

We work within the African and BAME communities creating the awareness on the rights of children enshrined in the United Nations Convention on the Rights of the Child and other international conventions and the UK legislation promoting the rights and welfare of children.

- ***Education, Research and Advisory Services***

Through education, research and advisory services, we create awareness of the African children's needs, improve policies and practices and develop healthy family relationships amongst African families. Activities include seminars, workshops, training, research and publishing reports; programmes for parents, policy makers, service providers, community leaders, faith organisations, community meetings, consultancy and advisory services. We also develop and deliver courses for practitioners in the social welfare field.

- ***Community Development***

We develop programmes in partnership with other organisations putting in place programmes and projects, which address the needs of children and families especially in the BAME community.

- ***Support Services for African and BME children, young people and families in crisis***

Through our effective early intervention services, we

work to support children, young people and families at the point of breakdown.

- ***NEI Centre for Parenting Education UK***

The New Era Initiative Centre for Parenting Education UK is our new arm in Parenting Education working across the United Kingdom. A specialist one stop-centre that provides a range of services for families and children. These are early intervention and preventive projects and programmes.

- ***Effective Parenting Initiative***

Projects and early invention services aimed at providing parental education for parents and caregivers struggling in their parental skills, this is NEI's landmark. We offer positive parenting skills, child protection awareness, health and wellbeing programmes, first aid training and education for parents and caregivers to reduce the number of children subject to child protection plans or being removed from their families and placed in the care.

Achievement Goal

- Parents and carers acquire positive knowledge in

improving parental skills

- Investing in early intervention and preventive projects to reduce child abuse

- Parents achieving better skills and knowledge to prevent removal of children from their care

- The community will gain a full understanding of the effects of child abuse and how to protect children

- Parents will receive support and information on child protection issues at the NEI Centre for Parenting Education

nei
New Era Initiative
EMPOWERMENT | DEVELOPMENT | SUSTAINABILITY

EFFECTIVE PARENTING